TICKET TO THE
WNBA FINALS

MARTIN GITLIN

45TH PARALLEL PRESS

Published in the United States of America by Cherry Lake Publishing Group
Ann Arbor, Michigan
www.cherrylakepublishing.com

Reading Adviser: Beth Walker Gambro, MS Ed., Reading Consultant, Yorkville, IL.

Photo Credits: © AP Photo/Pamela Smith, cover; © lrkhamster stock/Shutterstock, inside cover, 13, 19, 25, 29; © Nosyrevy/Shutterstock, 2, 3, 6, 10, 16, 23, 32; © Brocreative/Shutterstock, 5; © AP Photo/David J. Phillip, File, 7; © AP Photo/Michael Caulfield, 9; © Zuma Press, Inc. / Alamy Stock Photo, 11; © SPP Sport Press Photo. / Alamy Stock Photo, 12; © AP Photo/Kevork Djansezian, 15; © AP Photo/Brett Coomer/ASSOCIATED PRESS, 17; Lorie Shaull, via Wikimedia Commons, 18; © ZUMA Press Inc/Alamy Stock Photo, 21; © ZUMA Press Inc / Alamy Stock Photo, 22; Lorie Shaull from St Paul, United States, CC BY-SA 2.0 via Wikimedia Commons, 24; © SPP Sport Press Photo./Alamy Stock Photo, 27, 28

Copyright © 2026 by Cherry Lake Publishing Group

All rights reserved. No part of this book may be reproduced or utilized in any form or by any means without written permission from the publisher.

45th Parallel Press is an imprint of Cherry Lake Publishing Group.

Library of Congress Cataloging-in-Publication Data

Names: Gitlin, Marty author
Title: Ticket to the WNBA finals / Written by Martin Gitlin.
Other titles: Ticket to the Women's National Basketball Association finals
Description: Ann Arbor, Michigan : 45th Parallel Press, [2025] | Series: The big game | Audience: Grades 7-9 | Summary: "Who has won the WNBA finals? How did they make it happen? Filled with high-interest text written with struggling readers in mind, this series includes fun facts, intriguing stories, and captivating play-by-plays from this culmination of the WNBA season"-- Provided by publisher.
Identifiers: LCCN 2025009363 | ISBN 9781668963906 hardcover | ISBN 9781668965221 paperback | ISBN 9781668966839 ebook | ISBN 9781668968444 pdf
Subjects: LCSH: Women's National Basketball Association--History--Juvenile literature | Basketball for women--United States--History--Juvenile literature
Classification: LCC GV885.515.W66 G58 2025 | DDC 796.323082--dceng/23/20250426
LC record available at https://lccn.loc.gov/2025009363

Cherry Lake Publishing Group would like to acknowledge the work of the Partnership for 21st Century Learning, a Network of Battelle for Kids. Please visit Battelle for Kids online for more information.

Printed in the United States of America

Note from publisher: Websites change regularly, and their future contents are outside of our control. Supervise children when conducting any recommended online searches for extended learning opportunities.

Table of Contents

Introduction 4
History of the Game 8
Early Days, Big Moments 14
Modern Moments 20
Rising Stars 26

    ACTIVITY 30
    LEARN MORE 30
    GLOSSARY 31
    INDEX 32
    ABOUT THE AUTHOR 32

Introduction

The Women's National Basketball Association was born in 1996. It is also known as the WNBA. It is a women's professional basketball league. A new season begins every May.

Millions follow the National Basketball Association (NBA). That is a professional men's basketball league. From the start, the NBA promoted the WNBA. But the women received less attention. Crowds got smaller over the years.

Then it happened. Exciting new players joined the WNBA in 2024. Attendance soared. So did TV ratings. Fans poured into arenas. People began talking about the league.

The waiting is over and the big game is about to begin. Get ready, basketball fans!

The WNBA had its ups and downs. But the WNBA Finals have always been exciting. The 2 best teams play for the **championship** every October. That is the event that decides the league winner.

At first, it was just one game. It was called the WNBA Championship. It became a series of 3 games in 1998. It was renamed in 2001. Now it is the WNBA Finals. More games were added. Teams played 5 games. Excitement kept growing.

In 2025, 2 more games were added. A team must win 4 games out of 7 to win. Those games are exciting. Anything can happen. Teams are at their best. Fans watch every second.

Let the big games begin!

The Houston Comets won the first WNBA Championship in 1997. Point guard Kim Perrot celebrated the victory.

History of the Game

Women's basketball fans once had few options. Many watched college or high school teams. But there were no **professional athletes**. Those are athletes paid to play.

When the WNBA started in 1996, it was small. NBC is a TV network. It agreed to show WNBA games. Eight cities hosted teams.

Several top players signed up to compete. Included were superstars Sheryl Swoopes and Rebecca Lobo. A **draft** was held. That is where teams select top talent.

Soon came the moment fans craved. It was June 21, 1997. The referee tossed the ball. Lisa Leslie and Kym Hampton jumped for the tipoff. The first WNBA game was on.

This is the tipoff of the first WNBA game ever played in 1997. Lisa Leslie (right) played for the Los Angeles Sparks. Kym Hampton (left) played for the New York Liberty.

The early WNBA had big stars. They played for big cities. Its best player was Lisa Leslie. She played for the Los Angeles Sparks. The New York Liberty also had a superstar. That was Rebecca Lobo. Fans packed arenas to watch them.

The league added more stars. Cynthia Cooper joined the Houston Comets. The Seattle Storm signed Sue Bird. The Phoenix Mercury added Diana Taurasi.

But something was wrong. Attendance dropped. Interest lagged. The WNBA needed a spark. And it got one in 2024.

That was the year women's college basketball was hot. It had the sport's biggest superstar. Her name? Caitlin Clark. She had played college basketball for the University of Iowa.

In college, Clark was an amazing shooter. She was a great passer. Her team was on fire. It played for a college championship. Her games were **sellouts**. All the tickets were sold. TV ratings soared.

Sue Bird goes up for a basket. Superstar players have brought fans to the WNBA. They've made the Finals a must-watch event.

Clark joined the WNBA after college. She played for the Indiana Fever. Clark performed well. Three of her games drew 20,000 fans. Average league attendance rose 3,000 fans per game. More and more people are watching the Finals.

University of Iowa standout Caitlin Clark entered the WNBA in 2024. It sent the WNBA's popularity soaring.

Maya Moore was incredible. She played for Minnesota. Moore was a great dribbler. She made shots from all over the court. Moore played 8 seasons. And she averaged 19.3 points per game.

Her biggest moment arrived in 2013. The Minnesota Lynx were playing for the WNBA championship. Their opponent was the Atlanta Dream.

Moore was ready. She scored 23 points in the first game. Moore added 30 in Game 2. She scored 14 in Game 3. The Lynx won them all. They were WNBA champions.

They had Moore to thank for it. Moore knew she had to play her best. And she did.

AMAZING MOMENT

Early Days, Big Moments

In the WNBA, playing in the Finals brings pressure. Some players rise to perform their best. That's what Cynthia Cooper did. She dominated the Finals. Cooper played for the Houston Comets. That team won the first 4 WNBA Championships. Cooper was its best player in all of them.

Houston's streak ended in 2000. Houston beat New York in the Finals. Before 2005, the finals were best of 3 games. The Comets won the first game. Cooper worked well with teammate Sheryl Swoopes. They combined for 56 points in Game 2. They won that game and the championship with it.

The Houston Comets won every Final from 1997 to 2000. But they didn't win every game in the final tournament. New York Liberty star Teresa Weatherspoon made sure of that.

Star Cynthia Cooper dominated early WNBA Finals. She played for Houston.

The date was September 4, 1999. It was Game 2. Houston had already won Game 1. Another victory would clinch the title. Houston was winning by 1 point. Three seconds remained in the game.

Weatherspoon dribbled the ball. There was no time to set up a close shot. She heaved the ball 50 feet (15.2 meters). It was an almost impossible try. But it swished through the net. The Liberty had an incredible win. Weatherspoon was mobbed by teammates.

The Liberty lost the next game. The Comets got the championship. But fans would never forget that moment. Neither would Weatherspoon.

When more games were added in 2005, teams had more chances to win. Incredible shots could keep the series going. That's what happened 8 years after Weatherspoon's big moment.

The Phoenix Mercury were in trouble. It was the 2007 Finals. They were playing the Detroit Shock. One more loss and Phoenix was doomed.

Game 2 in the 1999 WNBA Finals was a surprise. Teresa Weatherspoon was the star.

Phoenix was losing 76–75. The clock was ticking. It was down to 20 seconds. They had to make a shot.

Phoenix player Cappie Pondexter dribbled slowly. Suddenly she cut to the left. Pondexter leaped forward. She shot the ball. It bounced off the backboard. And it dropped through the basket.

That put Phoenix ahead. The team hung on to win. They then won Game 5. They were champions. Pondexter had made it possible.

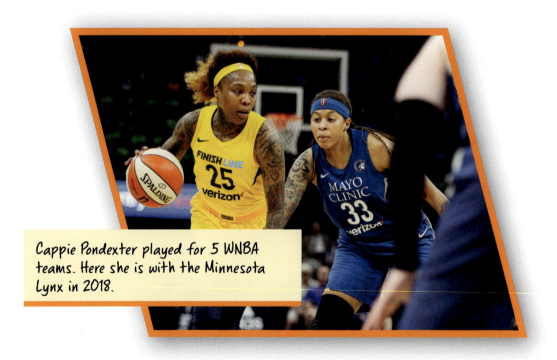

Cappie Pondexter played for 5 WNBA teams. Here she is with the Minnesota Lynx in 2018.

Turning teams around usually takes time. They don't go from bad to good overnight. But sometimes it happens. It did for the 2003 Detroit Shock.

The 2002 team was terrible. The Shock won 9 games. And they lost 23. But one coach made a difference. His name was Bill Laimbeer. The Shock began to play better after he took over.

They were ready to win in 2003. The Shock finished with a 25-9 record. And they kept winning in the playoffs. They next played for the WNBA title. And they beat the Los Angeles Sparks.

It was over. The Shocks had shocked the world. And they did it in 1 year.

WAY BACK WHEN

Modern Moments

It was 2016. And Minnesota was a **dynasty**. That is a team that dominates for years. The Minnesota Lynx had won 3 titles in 5 seasons. Their main rival was the Los Angeles Sparks. The 2 teams were fighting for the 2016 title.

It was Game 5. A sellout crowd packed the arena. The Lynx were down by 1 point. Just 20 seconds remained in the game. Lynx star Maya Moore shot the ball. It went through the net.

It seemed the Lynx would win. But Sparks standout Nneka Ogwumike had other ideas. She refused to let her team lose.

Ogwumike stood 6-foot-2 (188 centimeters). She knew her role. It was to **rebound**. That is when you catch the ball after a missed shot. So she stood near the basket. And she waited.

Game 5 of the 2016 Finals may have been the greatest WNBA game ever.

Sparks star Nneka Ogwumike rebounded an important basket. It gave her team the win.

Her Sparks teammate Chelsea Gray missed. But Ogwumike snagged the ball. She took a shot. A Lynx player blocked it. Ogwumike caught the ball again. And she shot it again. This time it sank through the hoop. The Sparks were ahead by 1 point.

Just 3 seconds remained in the game. Lynx standout Lindsay Whalen heaved the ball. It went toward the basket. But it did not go in. The Sparks were champions.

But that didn't end the Minnesota dynasty. Minnesota came back the next year. They beat Los Angeles. They won the 2017 Finals. That was the end of their run. They didn't make it back to the Finals until 2024. They lost to New York.

The Las Vegas Aces may be the next dynasty on the rise. They made it to the Finals in 2020. They lost that year. But they are a team to watch. They won the Finals in 2022. They made it back in 2023. They were up against the New York Liberty to take the title.

Las Vegas's A'ja Wilson sets up for a shot.

Game 4 was in New York. Nearly 17,000 fans packed the arena. Just 90 seconds remained. Las Vegas star A'ja Wilson made a shot. That put her team ahead 70–64.

New York refused to lose. Courtney Vandersloot hit a 3-pointer. Then teammate Sabrina Ionescu scored. It was 70–69.

One second remained. Vandersloot took another shot. It could have won the game. But it did not go in. Time ran out. And the Las Vegas Aces were champions again.

Most athletes hope for long careers. But most players average only 3- to 5-year careers. Those who play 10 years are lucky.

Then there is Diana Taurasi. She arrived in the WNBA in 2004. Taurasi was 22 years old. Taurasi was drafted by the Phoenix Mercury.

She was taken with the first pick. But nobody expected a 20-year career. Yet Taurasi was still playing in 2024. She was the top scorer in league history. Taurasi often averaged at least 20 points per game.

Taurasi even made the WNBA All-Star team in 2024. She did that at age 42! No player in WNBA history had ever made such an impact. Taurasi retired in 2025.

Rising Stars

Some stars burst onto the court out of college. Others shine brighter as time go on. They may be future legends.

Caitlin Clark and Angel Reese

Caitlin Clark revived the WNBA. That was in 2024. But she was not alone. Other young stars joined her. Perhaps the best was Angel Reese. She plays for the Chicago Sky.

Clark and Reese were **rivals** in college. That means they had a history of competing against each other. Both wanted to be the best. Reese averaged nearly 14 points per game in her **rookie** season in the WNBA. A rookie is a first-year player. She also averaged 13 rebounds per game. That is incredible.

Clark and Reese felt pressure. It showed when their teams met. The Indiana Fever hosted the Chicago Sky on June 1, 2024. Reese made only 2 of 9 shots. Clark hit only 4 of 9. Neither played well.

Angel Reese (center) is an impressive young WNBA star.

27

Rickea Jackson

The big spotlight in 2024 was on Clark. A smaller one shone on Reese. Other rookies received little notice. Among them was Rickea Jackson. Jackson played for the Los Angeles Sparks.

Jackson was just 23 years old. But she performed like a **veteran**. That is an experienced player. Jackson struggled early. Her shots often bounced off the rim.

Suddenly, Jackson started playing better. She averaged 16 points during her last 23 games. No rookie was better. Not even Clark and Reese.

Rickea Jackson (right) provided a spark for the Sparks in 2024.

Most fans love the **dunk**. That is when a player jumps high and slams the ball through the basket. It happens many times a game in the NBA. But dunks are rare in the WNBA.

★ The basket is 10 feet (3 m) from the floor. That is the same as in the NBA. Some believe the WNBA should lower the basket.

★ Only 8 WNBA players dunked in 27 years. NBA teams sometimes dunk that many times in 1 game.

★ The first WNBA player to dunk was Los Angeles Sparks superstar Lisa Leslie. She did it in 2002. She dunked again in 2005.

★ Candace Parker was the shortest player to dunk. Parker was 6-foot-4 (193 cm).

A BIT OF TRIVIA

Activity

Fantasy basketball is fun. It involves learning about the best players in the sport.

First, print out the statistics of every WNBA team. Learn which players on teams are the best scorers. Wait until a few weeks before the WNBA season begins.

Plan a draft for that time. Invite your friends and family members. Try to draft at least 5 players. The draft should have 10 rounds. Each player will draft 1 WNBA player in each round.

The WNBA usually plays about 2 games a week. Keep track of how many points each WNBA player scores when the season starts. Those points go to the fantasy player who drafted that WNBA player. The fantasy player with the most points at the end of the season wins.

Learn More

BOOKS

Anderson, Josh. *Indiana Fever.* Minneapolis, MN: Lerner Publishing, 2025.

Gerstner, Joanne C. *Diana Taurasi.* Lake Elmo, MN: Focus Readers, 2022.

Hicks, Ellen. *Caitlin Clark: Basketball Dreams Come True.* Oro Valley, AZ: TalesTold Publishing, 2024.

WEBSITES

Search these online sources with an adult.

Women's National Basketball Association facts for kids | Kiddle

WNBA Format Explained video | Snowman Sports Media
   WNBA website

Glossary

championship (CHAM-pee-uhn-ship) event that determines the winner in a league or sport

draft (DRAFT) annual selection by teams of top college talent

dunk (DUHNK) basketball throw from above the rim

dynasty (DIYE-nuh-stee) team that dominates for several years

professional athletes (pruh-FESH-nuhl ATH-leets) athletes who are paid to play

rebound (REE-bownd) catching the ball off a missed shot

rivals (RIYE-vuhlz) teams or players that have a history of competition

rookie (RUH-kee) first-year professional player

sellouts (SEL-owts) events in which all tickets are sold

veteran (VEH-tuh-ruhn) an experienced athlete

Index

A
activities, 30
amateur athletics, 8, 12
Atlanta Dream, 13

B
Bird, Sue, 10–11

C
Chicago Sky, 26–27
Clark, Caitlin, 12, 26
coaches, 19
college basketball players, 12
Cooper, Cynthia, 10, 14–15

D
Detroit Shock, 18–19
dunking, 29

F
fans, 4, 6, 10, 12, 29–30
fantasy basketball, 30

H
Hampton, Kym, 8–9
height, 29
Houston Comets, 7, 10, 14–16

I
Indiana Fever, 12, 26–27

J
Jackson, Rickea, 28

L
Laimbeer, Bill, 19
Las Vegas Aces, 23–24
Leslie, Lisa, 8–10, 29
Lobo, Rebecca, 8, 10
Los Angeles Sparks, 9–10, 15, 19–23, 28–29

M
Minnesota Lynx, 13, 20–23
Moore, Maya, 13, 20–21

N
National Basketball Association (NBA), 4–6, 8, 29
New York Liberty, 9–10, 14, 16–17, 24

O
Ogwumike, Nneka, 20–23

P
Parker, Candace, 29
Perrot, Kim, 7
Phoenix Mercury, 10, 16, 18, 25
Pondexter, Cappie, 18
popularity and ratings, 6, 10, 12, 20, 26
professional sports leagues, 6, 8, 29

R
rebounds, 22–23, 26
Reese, Angel, 26–27
rising stars, 12, 26–28

S
Seattle Storm, 10–11
Swoopes, Sheryl, 8, 14

T
Taurasi, Diana, 10, 25

V
Vandersloot, Courtney, 24

W
Weatherspoon, Teresa, 14–17
Whalen, Lindsay, 23
Wilson, A'Ja, 24
WNBA Finals, 4–6, 14
  dynasties, 14–16, 20–23
  games, 7, 12–14, 16, 18–24
  popularity, 11–12, 20, 26
Women's National Basketball Association (WNBA)
  history, 6–12, 29
  schedule, 6, 30
  teams, 7–26, 28, 30

About the Author

Martin Gitlin is an educational book author based in Connecticut. He won more than 45 awards as a newspaper sportswriter from 1991 to 2002. Included was a first-place award from the Associated Press for his coverage of the 1995 World Series. He has had more than 200 books published since 2006. Most of them were written for students.